STAR WARS™

THE ADVENTURES OF BB-8

Written by David Fentiman

Penguin
Random
House

Written and Edited by David Fentiman
Project Art Editor Owen Bennett
Pre-Production Producer Marc Staples
Senior Producer Alex Bell
Managing Editor Sadie Smith
Managing Art Editor Ron Stobbart
Art Director Lisa Lanzarini
Publisher Julie Ferris
Publishing Director Simon Beecroft

For Lucasfilm
Editorial Assistant Samantha Holland
Executive Editor Jonathan W. Rinzler
Image Archives Stacey Leong
Art Director Troy Alders
Story Group Leland Chee, Pablo Hidalgo, and Rayne Roberts

First American Edition, 2016
Published in the United States by DK Publishing
345 Hudson Street, New York, New York 10014

Page design copyright © 2016 Dorling Kindersley Limited
DK, a Division of Penguin Random House LLC
16 17 18 19 20 10 9 8 7 6 5 4 3 2 1
001–280584–June/2016

© & TM 2016 LUCASFILM LTD.

A catalog record for this book is available from the Library of Congress.

ISBN 978-1-4654-5103-3 (Hardback)
ISBN 978-1-4654-5102-6 (Paperback)

DK books are available at special discounts when purchased in bulk for sales promotions,
premiums, fund-raising, or educational use. For details, contact: DK Publishing Special
Markets, 345 Hudson Street, New York, New York 10014 .
SpecialSales@dk.com

Printed and bound in China

A WORLD OF IDEAS:
SEE ALL THERE IS TO KNOW

www.dk.com
www.starwars.com

Contents

BB-8

The galaxy is full of droids.
There are big ones, small
ones, helpful ones, and
dangerous ones.

One of these droids is named
BB-8. BB-8 is an astromech
droid. Astromechs help
starpilots fly their ships
through space.

BB-8 belongs to Poe Dameron.
Poe is the bravest pilot in the
Resistance. The Resistance is
a group that protects the galaxy
from the evil First Order.

The First Order

The First Order wants to conquer the galaxy. Poe and the other members of the Resistance must stop it. The Resistance is led by General Leia.

Many years ago, Leia and her brother, Luke Skywalker, defeated the evil Galactic Empire.
The members of the Empire who escaped became the First Order.
Now the First Order wants revenge!

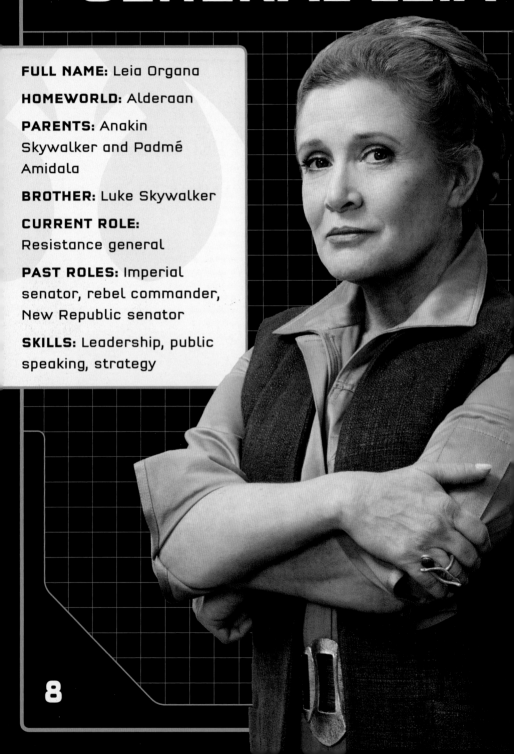

›GENERAL LEIA

FULL NAME: Leia Organa

HOMEWORLD: Alderaan

PARENTS: Anakin Skywalker and Padmé Amidala

BROTHER: Luke Skywalker

CURRENT ROLE: Resistance general

PAST ROLES: Imperial senator, rebel commander, New Republic senator

SKILLS: Leadership, public speaking, strategy

General Leia at the Resistance base

PROFILE:

- Leia fought bravely in the war against the Empire.

- She has now formed a new group to defend the galaxy from the First Order. This group is known as the Resistance.

- Leia's brother, Luke Skywalker, disappeared many years ago. Leia is trying to find him. She hopes that Luke will help her.

The village

BB-8 and Poe fly to the planet
Jakku to meet a man named
Lor San Tekka. Lor is an
explorer who has a map that
the Resistance needs. The map
shows where Luke Skywalker is.

Lor gives Poe the map, but then the First Order attacks Lor's village and takes Poe prisoner. Just before he is captured, Poe gives the map to BB-8. The brave little droid escapes into the desert.

In the desert

After Poe gets captured, BB-8
is left on his own. He is stuck
in Jakku's hot desert, with no
idea which way to go.

All BB-8 can do is roll toward the horizon, and hope to find someone who will help him.

BB-8 does not realize that he is being watched. A hungry creature called a nightwatcher worm is following him. Luckily, droids aren't very tasty, and it leaves him alone.

Meeting Rey

BB-8 is rolling through the
desert, trying to find help.
Suddenly he gets caught in
a net. A grouchy scavenger
named Teedo has grabbed him!

Teedo likes to take droids apart to steal their technology. Another scavenger named Rey hears BB-8's frightened beeping, and she rushes over to rescue him. Rey agrees to take BB-8 to a town called Niima Outpost.

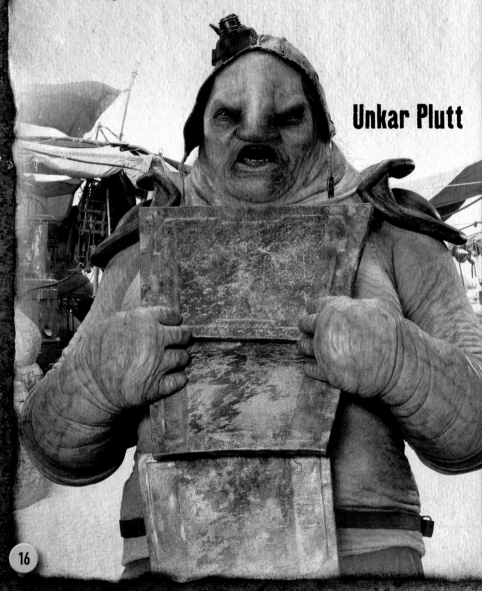

Welcome To
NIIMA OUTPOST

Niima can be a confusing place, so here is a guide for new arrivals.

Unkar Plutt

RULE NUMBER 1

Get scavenging. You will have to go into the Starship Graveyard and bring back technology to trade.

RULE NUMBER 2

Carry a blaster. Jakku is dangerous, with lots of hungry monsters and gangs of thieves. You will need to protect yourself.

RULE NUMBER 3

No fighting! Constable Zuvio will arrest anyone who makes trouble.

RULE NUMBER 4

Don't upset Unkar Plutt. Unkar is Niima's biggest, meanest junk boss. He has a gang of thugs that he sends after people who make him angry.

Constable Zuvio

Escape!

At Niima Outpost, BB-8 and Rey are chased by First Order stormtroopers. They run into an ex-stormtrooper named Finn. He is also being chased by the First Order.

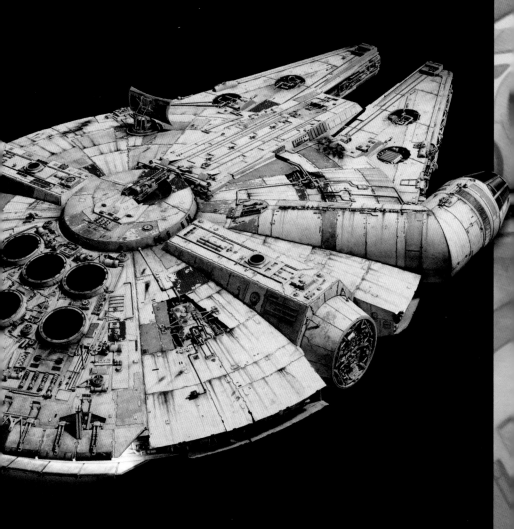

Together, BB-8, Rey, and Finn steal an old starship named the *Millennium Falcon*, and escape from Jakku. They get attacked by First Order ships, but Finn shoots the enemy down!

Han and Chewbacca

Just when Rey and Finn think they are safe, the *Millennium Falcon* breaks down! They are left floating helpless in space.

While Rey and Finn try to fix it, an enormous cargo ship appears. It swallows the *Millennium Falcon* whole!

The cargo ship belongs to Han Solo and Chewbacca. They are two legendary smugglers who used to own the *Millennium Falcon*.

Gangsters

BB-8 is nervous about Han and
Chewie, but it turns out they
are friendly. They are very happy
to have their old ship back.

Suddenly some gangsters board Han's cargo ship. They are enemies of Han and Chewie! The scary Guavians wear red, and the scruffy Kanjiklub wear black.

There is a big battle, but BB-8 and his friends escape on the *Millennium Falcon*. Han takes a look at the map BB-8 is carrying. Half of it is missing!

Maz's castle

Han and Chewie think that they should get some help. They take BB-8, Finn, and Rey to visit an old friend of theirs named Maz. Maz is a pirate who lives in a castle.

Maz's castle is very old.
It stands next to a lake on the
planet Takodana. The castle
is full of pirates and smugglers.
BB-8 has never seen so many
aliens in one place before.

BATTLE AT MAZ'S!

Rey and BB-8 are exploring Maz's castle. Rey finds herself being drawn toward the castle's dark basement.

Rey enters a mysterious room, and has a strong vision. She realizes that she has strange powers. Rey is confused and runs out of the castle, into the forest. BB-8 follows after her.

Suddenly BB-8 and Rey hear a noise. It's the First Order! They have come to attack the castle and capture BB-8.

The castle has been destroyed, and stormtroopers are everywhere. Finn, Han, and Chewie try to fight back.

The Resistance has arrived! Its X-wings battle the First Order's TIE fighters.

Kylo Ren is the First Order's greatest warrior. He wears a mask and carries a lightsaber. Kylo attacks Rey in the forest and takes her prisoner.

The First Order retreats, and General Leia arrives in a transport. She meets with Han, Finn, Chewie, and BB-8. They realize that Rey has been captured.

Battle plan

After the battle at Maz's castle, BB-8 and his friends travel to the Resistance base on the planet D'Qar.

Rey has been captured, and the First Order has revealed its powerful secret weapon. It is known as the Starkiller.

The Starkiller can destroy an entire star system. With this weapon, the First Order will be able to conquer the galaxy!

The Resistance has to destroy the Starkiller. The Resistance pilots put together a daring plan to attack it.

PILOT'S LOG:
JESS PAVA

🔶 Blue and Red squadrons are going to attack the Starkiller. I'm not nervous. Our X-wings are faster and stronger than the First Order's TIE fighters.

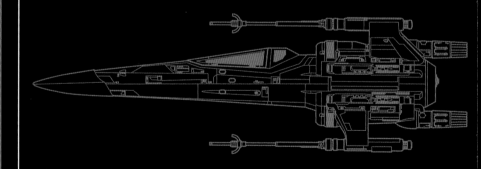

☮ My code name will be
Blue Three. Commander
Poe is going to lead us,
and he always brings us victory.

☮ BB-8 has come
back to the
Resistance base.
I'm glad to see him.
I thought he had
been destroyed.

☮ I should get some sleep. It's
going to be a big day tomorrow!

Reunited with Poe

BB-8 hasn't seen Poe Dameron since Poe was captured on Jakku. The Resistance must have rescued him, and BB-8 is very happy to see Poe again.

BB-8 will fly in Poe's X-wing for the attack on the Starkiller.

BB-8 has been in many battles before, so he is not scared.

Poe is going to fly a special black-and-orange X-wing, named *Black One*. This is BB-8's favorite ship.

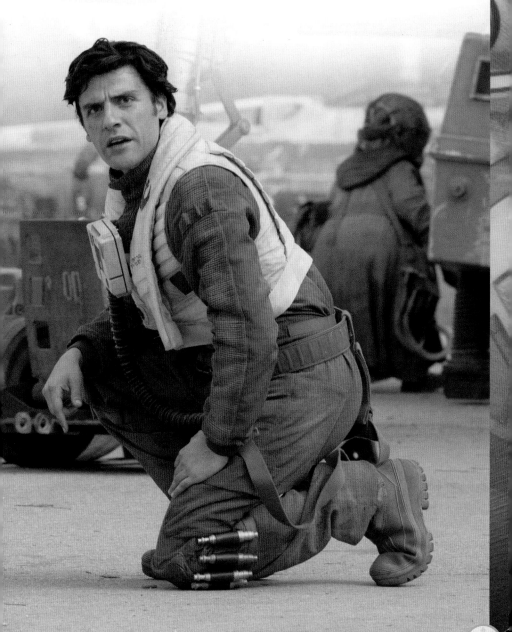

C-3PO and R2-D2

At the Resistance base,
BB-8 meets two very
famous droids,
C-3PO and R2-D2.
They both once
belonged to
Luke Skywalker,
General Leia's
brother.

C-3PO and R2-D2
helped Luke and
Leia defeat the
evil Empire.

After the war, Luke disappeared and R2-D2 went silent. R2 has been shut down ever since.

C-3PO serves Leia as her assistant. He always talks to R2 even though R2 never talks back!

BB-8's friends

There are many droids serving with BB-8 in the Resistance. They each do different jobs, but they are all important.

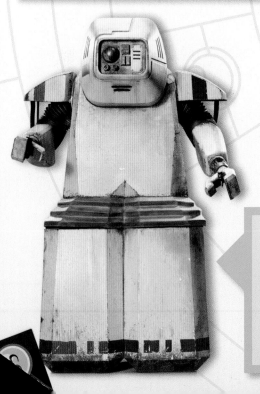

NAME: PZ-4CO
CLASS: Communications droid (translates messages)

NAME: B-U4D
CLASS: Loading droid (maintains X-wing fighters)

NAME: M9-G8
CLASS: Astromech droid (helps starship pilots)

NAME: GA-97
CLASS: Spy droid (keeps watch for the First Order)

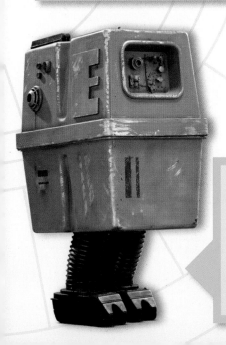

NAME: 4B-EG-6
CLASS: Power droid (a big walking battery)

Attacking the Starkiller

The Resistance pilots fly to attack the Starkiller. BB-8 joins Poe in his special X-wing starfighter.

Rey manages to escape from her cell, and she meets up with Han, Chewie, and Finn. They attack the Starkiller on the ground, while Poe and his pilots battle the First Order's TIE fighters.

BB-8 is very brave. After a hard battle, the Resistance finally manages to destroy the Starkiller.

Poe and BB-8 fly back to the Resistance base. BB-8 is happy to still be in once piece!

Victory!

Back at the Resistance base, everyone is happy that the Starkiller has been destroyed. It was a tough battle, and some of the Resistance did not return. Finn was wounded, but Rey rescued him.

R2-D2 wakes up, and realizes that
he has the missing half of BB-8's
map. They put the map back
together. Now they know where
Luke is! Rey is going to find him.
Everyone watches as she takes
off in the *Millennium Falcon*.

Quiz

1. What kind of droid is BB-8?

2. Who does BB-8 belong to?

3. Who does Rey rescue BB-8 from?

4. What planet is Maz's castle on?

5. What is the name of
   Poe's special X-wing?

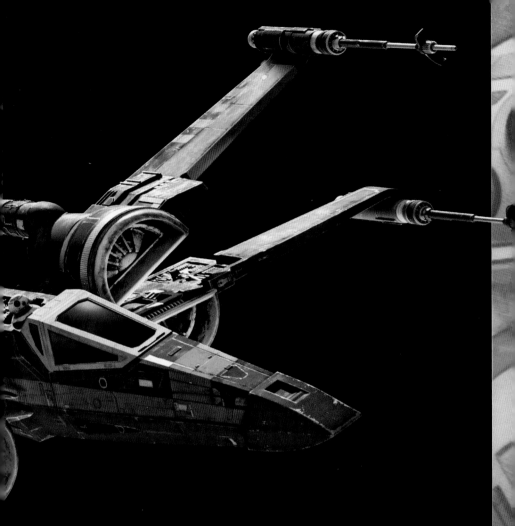

6. What is the First Order's secret weapon?

7. What is Jess Pava's code name?

8. Which droid serves as Leia's assistant?

9. Who has the missing half of BB-8's map?

Answers on page 48

Glossary

Blaster
A weapon that fires glowing bolts of energy

Conquer
To take control of something using force

Droid
A robot

Empire
An evil group that once ruled the galaxy, but which was destroyed

Explorer
Someone who travels to places that no one has been to before

First Order
A new army formed by the survivors of the Empire

Leadership
The ability to lead people well

Mysterious
Strange, or hard to explain

Nervous
To feel worried or scared

Resistance
A group created to protect the galaxy from the First Order

Retreat
To escape from a battle or situation

Reunited
When things that were once together, but then separated, are put back together again

Scavenger
Someone who searches through worthless junk to find useful things

Senator
A member of a senate (a type of government)

Smuggler
Someone who transports illegal goods

Starkiller
A giant secret weapon built on an icy planet by the First Order

Technology
Equipment made using scientific knowledge

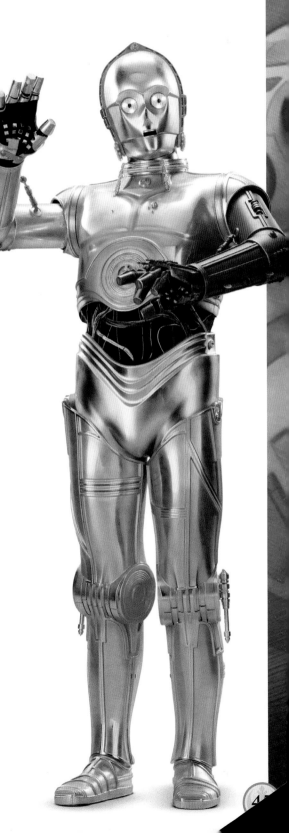

Guide for Parents

This book is part of an exciting four-level reading series for children, developing the habit of reading widely for both pleasure and information. These chapter books have a compelling main narrative to suit your child's reading ability. Each book is designed to develop your child's reading skills, fluency, grammar awareness, and comprehension in order to build confidence and engagement when reading.

Ready for a *Level 2* book

YOUR CHILD SHOULD

- be familiar with using beginning letter sounds and context clues to figure out unfamiliar words.
- be aware of the need for a slight pause at commas and a longer one at periods.
- alter his/her expression for questions and exclamations.

A valuable and shared reading experience

For many children, reading requires much effort, but adult participation can make this both fun and easier. So here are a few tips on how to use this book with your child.

TIP 1 Check out the contents together before your child begins:

- read the text about the book on the back cover.
- flip through the book and stop to chat about the contents page together to heighten your child's interest and expectation.
- make use of unfamiliar or difficult words on the page in a brief discussion.
- chat about the nonfiction reading features used in the book, such as headings, captions, lists, or charts.

TIP 2 Support your child as he/she reads the story pages:

• give the book to your child to read and turn the pages.

• where necessary, encourage your child to break a word into syllables, sound out each one, and then flow the syllables together. Ask him/her to reread the sentence to check the meaning.

• when there's a question mark or an exclamation point, encourage your child to vary his/her voice as he/she reads the sentence. Demonstrate how to do this if it is helpful.

TIP 3 Chat at the end of each page:

• ask questions about the text and the meaning of the words used. These help to develop comprehension skills and awareness of the language used.

A FEW ADDITIONAL TIPS

• Always encourage your child to try reading difficult words by themselves. Praise any self-corrections, for example, "I like the way you sounded out that word and then changed the way you said it, to make sense."

• Try to read together everyday. Reading little and often is best. These books are divided into manageable chapters for one reading session. However, after 10 minutes, only keep going if your child wants to read on.

• Read other books of different types to your child just for enjoyment and information.

Series consultant, **Dr. Linda Gambrell**, Distinguished Professor of Education at Clemson University, has served as President of the National Reading Conference, the College Reading Association, and the International Reading Association.

Index

Answers to the quiz on pages 42 and 43:
1. astromech droid 2. Poe Dameron 3. Teedo 4. Takodana
5. *Black One* 6. the Starkiller 7. Blue Three 8. C-3PO 9. R2-D2

3-21